Visions of God

Expressions of a Modern Prodigal

by Rick Rapp

PublishAmerica
Baltimore

ISBN: 1-4137-8426-7
PUBLISHED BY PUBLISHAMERICA, LLLP
www.publishamerica.com
Baltimore

Printed in the United States of America

*To God...my Father in heaven,
my family, friends, and teachers who
held me along this journey of faith
towards healing, expression and boldness.*

Contents

Foreword

A young man, or woman for that matter, must sometimes experience great trials of their heart, spirit, and faith. Such is the practice of maturation in the world of God's creation. The story to follow begins in much the same way as that of the biblical prodigal son...with exuberance and expectation of opportunity, grandeur and deep-rooted self-sufficiency:

I am...

I am anxious and hopeful beyond my means.
I wonder when I am going to burst.
I hear about possibilities.
I see opportunities.
I pretend that I have secured my future.
I feel that my potential is immeasurable.
I touch unexplored territory.
I worry that I might miss out on life.
I weep when I can't get where I want to go.
I understand that I can't accomplish everything.
I say what others need to hear.
I dream, I think, and I pray about my future.
I try, and will always try to live a decent life.
I hope that I can make a difference in this world.
I am anxious and hopeful beyond my means.

I wrote that poem on September 3rd, 1995 at the age of fifteen. Little did I know the path that I would take over the ten years that would follow those simple, youthful thoughts! Married at the age of nineteen to a woman that I loved, yet oddly did not know *how* to love in both my spiritual and human immaturity. The marriage lasted five years during which time I lived a life of passivity, separation from God, from myself, from my dreams, all to try and please a woman that I was incapable of pleasing in my mortality.

She was and is a wonderful woman, but I was weak and allowed the relationship and my masculine heart to crumble, away from the support of

God, family, and friends. The verses compiled in the pages to come represent the journey of one young man through the ending of a marriage, deep brokenness, God's forgiveness, a faith reborn, and new perspectives on life, creation, and Eve. It is my deep hope and prayer that God may use these words to help other men find and express themselves to the Father, the world, and the women in their lives. So too may it be possible for women to find this work to be a window into a man's heart, his wounds, and his healing.

Part 1 - Man Broken

Each man reaches a point
on his path in life where he no
longer can proceed…and falls
to his knees in the weakness
he has so long denied.

Emasculated

Wild at heart, broken in spirit...hurt
Exposed for the man that I am not
Pride gives way to tears, ego to fears
emasculated by my mortality.

Where are you now God, my God?
Speak to me! Say something! Say anything...anything
I, the weakened hypocrite demand...answer me!
emasculated by my selfishness.

When did the adventure give way to hell?
How did I stray so far from Love?
My soul screams for the freedom of your grace
emasculated by my self-indulgence.

My wild heart is dying, slowly, slowly.
Bring me back into the fold, a sheep
lost, lost am I, my fleece stained red
emasculated by my ignorance.

Seek ye first the kingdom of God
and thine manhood will return in His power.
Let the adventure resume, glorious
true masculinity by humble faith.

Swordsman and Healer

O the moment of consequence when
a man gazes upon his shattered
self, prideful self broken on the floor
under the feet of Him, the true
owner of his soul, replaced by
his Eve, his greed, and wretched sin!

His heart spews bloodied cries
from the wound of reclamation.
The devil's breathe still warm
despite his hurried flight from
the Christ, the hunter of souls
lost within themselves.

To this day men draw lots
for a shred of Jesus' robe
to tourniquet their wounded hearts,
pierced by nails as He took
their sins to hell...
bleeding until man lets Him in.

Swordsman and Healer, he pierces
and renews, heals and gives rest
to those who crucify Him
every moment, every day, such is
the cycle of man, of mortality...
such is the power of grace!

"Come, let us return to the Lord.
He has torn us to pieces
but he will heal us;
he has injured us
but he will bind up our wounds"
(Hos. 6:1)

Young Man Seeking

A wind, mighty wind rushes
through the chasm deep in each
young man's soul, his spirit
aching for something unknown
too afraid to express his need
too modernly masculine to cry.

He walks down tree-lined paths
A coat warming him despite
the summer heat, an inner frigidity
sad, so sad, weakness maybe?
Too young to know the difference
too naïve to realize strength.

Temporary triumphs overcome
by the need for more and more
adventure, praise, love sought
from imperfect, unknowing lovers,
brothers, sisters, friends, insufficient!
The wind howls, dust holds firm.

He drinks, he runs, he earns,
he spends, he lifts, he falls,
an obligatory cycle of youth...
post-teen manhood summarized.
Still a hole, still a puzzle
incomplete...pieces missing.

His failure is the search
for a single piece, hourglass shape
curvaceous, yet not enough...
as he soon realizes, still
longing, seeking, pursuing in
directions false and deceiving.

He walks down a pew-lined aisle
a coat removed in the warmth
of smiles, of hope, of peace
that he does not understand
but realizes nonetheless the
perfect fulfillment of Christ!

Denial

My eyes follow her, mind racing
      I do not know the man!
My mouth and heart silent as Eve reaches out
      I tell you I do not know him!
Children crave my lap not offered
      I do not know him!

...and the rooster crows...

Free-Written Thoughts 1

Wandering through the wilderness
the emotions of men
so convoluted and confusing
with each passing day
seeking validation in myself,
from you, from her,
seeking truth in dark woods,
where is it? Why are we
so complex and challenging?
I want to solve, to fix,
but I can't because I
don't know how I work,
how I was made, but
I have to believe this complexity
comes from something, someone
higher than myself...
And there is peace in that
thought, maybe because it
is such a simple solution
when I've buried myself in
the details of myself that
confuse me more than any
woman ever could.
Faith...will it bring me out...
out of the wild, or maybe
leave me here on a path
where I can see myself
through the trees and maybe,
just maybe I will finally
rest in the shade.

Proverbs 3:5-6 - A lyric

Trust, believe, submit from the depths of your soul,
All that is you and all that you know,
To the One who molded you from clay and loving tears.

Forget what is trivial, meek, small, and mortal,
For that is what we understand…and what limits us.
It is our humanity and it is frail.

Take a breath and remember that it is a gift.
Let it fill you with the divine and the glorious.
Let it claim you, overwhelm you, break you.

Take a step and remember that there is a path.
Let it guide you over mountains high, through valleys low.
Let it take you always towards the rising sun.

Speak a word and remember His word, His book.
Let it flow freely into your heart and out of your lips.
Let it be heard, let it be felt, let it bring joy.

Listen for the simple, powerful, quiet utterances of God.
Hear what He says to you, seek what He wants from you,
Cry joyfully because He loves, truly loves.

"Trust in the Lord with all your heart
and lean not on your own understanding.
In all your ways acknowledge Him
and He will make your paths straight."
(Prov. 3:5-6)

Free Will

Every man has faith
but it may be in himself
entirely and not in God...
possibly a combination of
the two, where I think I am.

As the road narrows and
bottlenecks, all but the few
who are strong enough to exit
onto the straight and narrow...

How the stereotype of directions
and man's refusal to seek them
has become an accurate microcosm
for the macrocosm of faith...

Free will is not so freeing
and quite frustrating at that,
for men who can't gain control
of it despite their best efforts.

And so we return to the question of
whom a man's faith is in.

Man's Standstill

I've thought about journaling before
but never felt compelled to do so
as it seemed redundant and unproductive
after already analyzing twenty times over.

But tonight I write, ironically...
because I'm tired, sleepy yes, but
truly tired! So much weight on my mind
eventually wears through my armor...

and I crash.

Where emotions were, I'm complacent
Where questions were, I'm satisfied...
while still unsatisfied.
Where motivations were, I'm static.

It's not due to the actions or inactions
of others, rather simply my own fault
for letting machismo, pride, ego, and
mortal masculinity take root in my spirit.

I've pressured myself, overcommitted
in an instinctual desire to hold up the
earth, while balancing the moon on
my nose to impress unknown onlookers.

Despite what I should know
from my faith in Christ, I still
try too hard, boast too much, and
pray from proverbial street corners...

Sadly I know that all this is
natural for men and normal for me
and when men get this way, they
need time alone with God and themselves...

Time to think, pray, and vegetate
in front of large television screens
spewing random sports and news of
little real value to us...just a ritual.

It's about recuperation of the man
and it is necessary beyond words...
without occasional solitude our crashes
are severe and God's resting mechanism...

well...it is broken.

Could we act different to avoid this need
for solitary time? I dare say yes, but
it would surely render us the lesser man,
husband, and father, lacking in drive.

It is destructive to deny a man his time
and I know this from experience as
I lost my masculinity to a woman
from whom I am now divorced.

It wasn't her fault, rather mine
because I let it happen, let myself
deny and ignore my need for solitary
time with my heavenly Father.

But tonight I reclaim my spirit
as I wait for sleep to come and renew
me for the commitments of tomorrow
when all will be normal again.

So men, claim your time, recognize the need!
And women, let his spirit be free
in books, music, competition, and faith!
For there the heart of man finds renewal!

Questioning

Love your wife as Christ
loved the church...
I failed, failed, failed
to cultivate and nurture
Christ-like love, why? How?
Was I too complacent,
too passive, too weak,
too fake, macho fake,
too selfish, too selfless,
too overdrawn, too tired?
A little of each I think...
the hardest lesson I've yet learned
came at the expense of the love
of her who gave herself to me,
who mishandled the gift.
Maybe I was mis-held too but
I only can be responsible
for my own failures, and successes...
well, successes are credited to God.
So goes the mind of a man
down the intrinsic pathway
towards regret, then pain, then healing.

Insomnia

The darkness envelopes my eyes,
but they adjust...slowly...
for sleep does not come,
will not visit this room tonight.
While lying in darkness my
mind is brightly blazing with thoughts
unending...unending...unending...
and why?

Replaying successes and failures,
conversations past, conversations to come,
momentarily seeking God in prayer
until my mind wanders away
from His outstretched arms and the
ease that would soothe my mind
to sleep...but no, I can't escape...
and why?

Insomnia for me cannot be cured
by warm milk, nature sounds, or
pills that swallow easier than my pride
which seems to reach its gnarled fingers
into each of these convoluted paths
of thoughts. Oh to sleep and
dream of nothing! Mind at rest...
and why?

I read poems by Frost, by David,
by Solomon whom I imagine had
many sleepless nights as a man of
great wisdom. Did he know how to
shut off his brain, his thoughts?
Did his wisdom so exhaust him to sleep
while my lack of wisdom keeps me awake...
and why?

I am a complicated man,
a complicated, exhausted soul
and Lord...I need to sleep!

The Burdened Heart

Drop after drop hitting the bucket,
filling, more and more, heavy
with viscous burdens and the dirt
I cannot filter as the load crushes.

My faithful legs scream in pain,
loyal to my careless, reckless self.
Fix...help...resolve, must I?
Must I?

The yoke breaks, all pours out.
The whip of my ego strikes my
back in fearful rage, childish rage...
I cannot stand again.

Fingers run through my hair
wiping sweat from my brow,
tears and blood from my cheek.
They take hold of a yoke.

I watch as He fills the buckets,
my buckets, knees buckling, then...
holding strong. Strength beyond man.
He gestures me to my feet.

There sits his yoke, small, light
and buckets filled with purity
quenching the thirsty souls of men.
I raise the yoke with ease...peace.

He moves onto the homebound path
and I follow, regaining the strength
of my masculine heart, humbled heart,
for this yoke is easy, and this burden is light!

*"Come to me, all you who are weary and burdened,
and I will give you rest. Take my yoke upon you
and learn from me, for I am gentle and humble
in heart, and you will find rest for your souls. For
my yoke is easy and my burden is light."*
(Matt. 11:28-30)

Part 2 - Man Healing

Brokenness gives way to
a thirst deep in the soul
for healing waters, refreshing
the spirit and mending the
heart from shards to shape.

Psalms 119: 9-11 - The Seeker's Soul

Young men waver between paths,
the reed swaying dramatically
under miniscule breezes in life...
a goose losing its flock as
it gazes at its own reflection
in the glassy lake below.
Selfish, self-indulged is the
man without the empowering
brokenness of true Godly insight!

Such is gained not so fully
through Sunday school and a
"Jesus Loves Me, This I Know"
childhood of spiritual routine.
Rather it is borne in a man
when on his knees he finally
becomes Christ-like washing the feet
of God, washing with his tears
of forgiveness sought, mercy received!

It is now when man seeks
the guidance his life has lacked,
by returning to the dust-covered
book that has too long sat as
a bowl-covered candle on his shelf,
no light emanating from its ignored
pages, no peace filling the reader's,
the seeker's soul...until now when
man's midnight eyes squint over the words.

With time he will find this book to
be a refuge from the world that
makes him ache to see the Kingdom Glory
of which he reads each night.
From his mouth, words begin to flow
in conversation he is only capable
of having with his Father God.
He has passion received from the
overwhelming truths of the Word!

"How can a young man keep his way pure?
By living according to your word.
I seek you with all my heart;
do not let me stray from your commands.
I have hidden your word in my heart
that I might not sin against you."
(Psalms 119: 9-1)

2 Timothy 1:6-7 - A Lyric

Looking to the west
I see clouds engulfing
the mountains I've known
since the time I was young.
Mountains solid, mountains strong,
always on the edge
of my peaceful existence.

Those mountains are boldness
that I've only possessed
in brief mornings and evenings
of a life lived safely
on flattened plains, save
the momentary journey on
trails to the unknown peak.

On these heights He faced temptation.
On these heights He prayed for me.
On these heights He shared the kingdom.
On these heights He died for
the sinful meekness that
keeps me on the edge, afraid.

I venture there more often
now as I open my eyes
to what I had not been, to
the man I had not become,
and I have found Him there
in the blessings of the mountains.

Each day I yearn for those peaks
of humble confidence and mighty power,
yearn to share with men
the mountains they cannot see
through the clouds of their
deaths, their shrouded hearts.

"For this reason I remind you to
fan into flame the gift of God,
which is in you through the laying
on of my hands. For God did not
give us a spirit of timidity, but
a spirit of power, of love, and
of self-discipline."
(2 Tim. 1:6-7)

Message From God

You are a man, you're starting something new,
discovering what I have for you.

Be open, be aggressive, fight Satan
and your flesh. It is time for you
to step forward and humble yourself.

Fiercely pursue me.
You have a great heart, a
masculine heart, a spiritual heart.

Love it and love yourself!
How dare you not love yourself
As I love you...my creation!

I am proud of you!
Be passionate!

Job 8: 5-7 - A Lyric

With heavenward glare into brilliance blinding
the souls of men are sold to the light
in desperate cries for healing...Oh the pain,
the tedious aches of sinful consequence!

With salvation tears they have been written in the book.
An intense whitewash with holy intercession.
The Son speaks, the Father listens...
He, the Divine, is ready to respond.

Desperation melts and flows into the sea
of Hope and Humility. Warm waters bathe their spirits,
exposing new directions, new signs, new paths.
Oh the amorous feelings of men for dreams!

God lifts them from their ragged knees,
the storehouses, their hearts, stretch their seams.
A simple glimpse, a moment of clarity,
a heavenward look into eye opening brilliance.

"But if you will look to God
and plead with the Almighty,
if you are pure and upright,
even now he will rouse himself on your behalf
and restore you to your rightful place.
Your beginnings will seem humble,
so prosperous will your future be."
(Job 8:5-7)

The Path Back to Living

I find myself turning in the darkness,
moving towards a light, a glimmer,
that which is hope when I've been hopeless,
that which is joy when I've been sad.
There is laughter emanating from the light,
it echoes, rumbles, fills my dark space.
It makes me smile, makes the light brighter,
pulls me toward the unknown, yet familiar.

Warmth passes through my soul.
It thaws cold feelings and emotions.
There is some pain and confusion in this thawing
but it is good, so good!
The light begins to illuminate my space now,
casting a vague glow on images I remember.
Things, visions, memories, ideas flood my mind.

Before the darkness there was God, all-encompassing,
there was knowledge, discourse, music, and friendship.
I see these images coming forward, out of the darkness.
The light gets brighter, the images clearer,
the laughter louder, the warmth stronger,
the hope fuller, and the joy more complete.
Thank you God, and those dear to me,
I'm on the path back to living!

Ticking

Clock hands move perpetually
        towards the return of Him
who has saved me from myself
        and will save me from this world
and the mind-numbing tasks that
        make those clock hands slur...between seconds...

Perhaps I complain too much
        and fail to see God's presence
in lecture halls and household chores
        that distract me from adventurous mischief.
Consider it pure joy when you face
        trials of your patience and maturity...

Camping Trip

Young boy with a heavy pack
fishing pole in his hand.
Summer day, warm at the trailhead,
he follows his father away from
the car, all civilization, no fear,
his father is here.

Into the wilderness, miles ahead
not to return for days,
campfires, the lake, starry nights,
excitement with each climbing step.
Eyes upon his father's feet,
sweating in the summer heat.

Soon the boy feels the weight
of the pack upon his back,
aching legs whine for rest
and he cries to his father to stop.
Only a mile in, his father walks on,
fear sets in before he is gone.

Minutes later the ache has left,
maybe his body adjusted to the strain,
maybe he is trying to impress
his father with his "strength".
Not long before he cries again
and father stops to talk to him.

"We have miles to go but if we push,
we'll make it in time for the best
fishing, when the big ones are biting,
campfire beans and chocolate smores…
it is all there after this hiking day,
so let us get along on our way."

He then reaches down into the pack
of the boy and rearranges
all the contents, shifting and moving
and amazingly the load is lighter.
With refreshed legs and motivation
the young boy walks with inspiration.

The rest of the hike is hard, tough,
strain offset by beautiful scenes,
fearful disappearances of the father
'round corners in the trail ahead.
Always a guide, always leading,
conscious of what his son is needing.

The trail flattens, eases, and
through the trees sunlight reflected
off the lake, their destiny, their
home for the week, yet longer.
Tent raised, fire built, setting sun,
fishing until supper's done.

A young man returns to this memory
while sitting on a rock next to
an unfamiliar trail in life, lost,
tired, confused, yells into the wilderness...
on the trail ahead a man appears,
the father is here!

Romans 15:13 - A Lyric

The Sun begins to rise on the horizon
of my spirit, early beams illuminating
long darkened crevices, moans echoing
off the walls of my heart which begin
to soften as hope awakens.

Longings for warmth have driven
me eastward towards the sunrise, my God.
A journey without destination yet
peaceful and secure amidst obstacles
beyond me, beyond my mortality.

Each day, each moment, each breathe
the sunshine is brighter, warmer
exposing my soul to the joy
that brings tears that fall
with me to my knees

I was lost but now am found
was blind but now I see
a sheep scattered, a shepherd savior
Oh the comfort of His arms!
Don't let go...never let go!

*"May the God of hope fill you with all joy
and peace as you trust in him, so that you may
overflow with hope by the power of the Holy Spirit."
(Rom. 15:13)*

Newness

A new place, a new face
        on this soul starting over
with lessons learned
        battles past, battles present.
Fight the good fight!
        Go west young man!
Ask not what this country
        can do for you, rather...
ask what you can do
        to get it right this time.

Resolutions, New Years, new fears
        lose the weight of a sinful past
embrace the lightened load!
        Clean your dirty laundry,
clean your closet, free of skeletons.
        Tell the truth...to yourself
Run a mile everyday...
        in another man's shoes.
Love more, cry more
        smile for the simple joy of smiling.

Part 3 - Creation Speaking

With subtleties and nature
He calls to the healing soul
to look deeper, beyond what
eyes can see and ears can hear
for purpose...for life...for freedom!

Philippians 3:14 - A Lyric

The trees pass by slowly, rustling, ever
thinning, ever shortening, giving in to
altitude high. Lungs burning, sun shining,
a rocky trail beneath his feet, winding.

Chipmunks bicker and give chase in
the boughs overhead, mountain meadows give
glimpses of the peak, his goal.
Wildflowers bloom under exposed sky, blue.

Thoughts of life dissipate under the pressure
of nature's, of God's surrounding beauty.
He pauses to quench his thirst. Water and prayer.
The wind speaks through the treetops, magnificent.

He continues on, up the trail, heavenward,
towards his goal, the summit, his prize,
his joy. He emerges from the timberline.
The boulders stand in great admiration, silent.

Legs tired, shoulders weakened by the load,
spirit floating like the clouds above, past
false summits, temporary disappointment, he focuses.
An eagle soars over the valley below, deep.

As the noontime sun reaches its peak
so to does he, overwhelmed, overjoyed,
his goal achieved, purpose fulfilled, success.
He looks down at the trailhead below, a smile.

"I press on toward the goal to win the prize for
which God has called me heavenward in Christ Jesus."
(Phil. 3:14)

Aging

Frosty snow
      ...settles in my hair
as I walk
      ...to the library and
am reminded
      ...that aging is inevitable
      ...and faith is rewarded.

Lifted

I am lifted high to the heavens
where stars kiss my cheeks and
the angels wipe away my tears.
There I rest in the palm of Christ,
my Savior, my Provider, my love!
As I sleep He places me on the lap
of God, who sings lullabies to me
and covers me with clouds to warm me,
His child, His lost sheep, His love!

Little Tree

Little Tree
        Big Dreams
                Shallow Roots

My Place

I have a spot I like to sit
and write each Friday between
class and work. It is comfortable.
Am I a creature of habit?

I have found inspiration here
and so I return without doubt
of newfound words to describe the day.
Am I unique in any way?

I think each man has a place
that he claims his own regardless
of who may occupy it...or him.
Is there anything wrong with that?

Christ had the wilderness where
he would refresh his heart in
the presence of the Father.
Do I find that here?

I have music in my ears,
books left, window right, great view,
and it is peaceful amidst battles.
Will my place ever change again?

In the past I have claimed
rooms, easy chairs, parks, trails,
different, but the same...good!
Is God present in this place?

Of course He's here, but do I
let him share this moment with
me, or deny the gift it is?
If the Father speaks, will I hear?

People walk by the window below
not knowing they have shared this
moment of beauty with me.
What are they thinking?

Is it possible I am unique
because I observe
and yet not unique at all
because I observe?

The man on the grass lawn below
may be in his place...observing,
but is it different for him...
Is he praying too?

My place makes me philosophical.
His place could be relaxing,
thought-provoking, thought-inhibiting.
What is his need?

The great mastery of God
is His incomparable power to put
men in the place they need most to be.
Don't you agree?

Direction in Winter

Morning snow...
                    ...inches deep
Path covered...
                    ...still there.

Teardrop

A teardrop on the floor
of the sanctuary...
footprint of Christ!

Rocky Mountain Wild

On winter's day upon a trail
in Rocky Mountain Wild...
I found a rock near flowing stream
and rested there awhile.

The rushing water through breaks in snow
reminded me of my thirst...
for Him who made this wild so,
for Him I must seek first.

On the peaks above the wind blows through
making branches speak the truth...
and clap their hands the trees in tune,
their words my soul did soothe.

My eyes, they panned across the snow
through a heavy, wooded view...
and saw a pine cone fall below
its mother to start anew.

At this moment God spoke to me
with a gust of wind above...
"you've found your home in wilderness
young man that I do love."

Faith Road

I read a poem by Robert Frost
about two roads in the woods,
of which he chose the one less traveled
and found it to be good...

It made me think of my past paths
and my trend toward conformity,
the path that most men chosen have,
to avoid presumed abnormality...

The path more traveled by men and I
does have a share of dead ends,
but rather it acts so circular and
to the beginning it repeatedly sends...

It seems that God will bring men back
to the choice of faith or sigh
in the hopes we'll see past our eyes
and take the road, "less traveled by!"

Regarding Robert Frost's poem, "The Road Not Taken."

Part 4 - Closeness to God

A meeting place for two souls,
one immortal and eternal,
the other humbled and beginning anew
amidst blessings now recognized
for the grace and mercy they represent.

Romans 1:16-20 - A Lyric

At times a whisper softly, softly spoken…
at times resounding like echoes through canyons deep.
Unabashed, unrelenting is the epic of the Divine!
Salvation, sweet salvation from my meek mortality.
The written words explode in radiance, blinding,
humbling, purifying my rotten soul, freedom!

I believe! I believe! Praise God I believe!

It is true, it is real, the Christ, He is real
the cloak of pride and selfishness torn off!
The echoes and whispers fill my senses, His
simplicity, an oasis I can finally see, I
no longer ignore in my human desolation.
He is everywhere…He is…He simply is.

Since dust was gathered to dust, and all was good
He existed in His creation. Emanating the Divine
in grasses humble, waters deep, mountains majesty.
No man can deny, no man can ignore
The epic of the Divine, the truth, the presence
consumed in every mortal breath.

*"I am not ashamed of the gospel, because it is the power of God for the salvation
of everyone who believes: first for the Jew, then for the Gentile. For in the gospel
a righteousness from God is revealed, a righteousness that is by faith from first to
last, just as it is written: "The righteous will live by faith."*

*The wrath of God is being revealed from heaven against all the godlessness and
wickedness of men who suppress the truth by their wickedness, since what may
be known about God is plain to them, because God has made it plain to them.
For since the creation of the world God's invisible qualities--his eternal power and
divine nature--have been clearly seen, being understood from what has been
made, so that men are without excuse."*
(Rom. 1:16-20)

An Image

God
Man
Weak
Sin
Pain
Apart
Son of God Almighty above, comes to save
my weak, humbled and wounded heart
Heals
Grows
Tests
Trials
Prayer
Friend
Father
Husband
Son
Child
set

apart   through
   Jesus   Christ
To   be   passionate   and   wild!

A Prayer of Desire

Expose my mind Father
to the epiphany of
Your word.

Tear open the shackles
that bind me from
Your guidance.

Each day brighter than
those lived far from
Your embrace.

Advise my humbled heart
with the power of
Your wisdom.

Push my potential into
the pure reality of
Your glory!

Fill my soul with
the incomparable knowledge of
Your teaching.

Sing with lyrics breathed
to fill me with
Your joy.

Open the gates so
I may live in
Your freedom!

*"Then you will know the truth
and the truth will set you free."*
(John 8:32)

Least of These

Dirty face and shopping cart
brings Christ to mind
      ...as I buy an extra cup of coffee.

I See Jesus

As I kneel in quiet solitude
on knees broken by the strain
of past self-insufficiency...
I see Jesus sitting on my bed.

As the congregation rises, there
is a face buried in calloused
hands shaken by his sobs...
I see Jesus looking eye to eye.

Christian fish and carpenter stickers
on a bumper rusted through
this world's greed and consequence...
I see Jesus riding shotgun.

A fervent prayer from the peak
of his mountain as he sees his
wake of destroyed love and faith below...
I see Jesus clearing His temple.

Hearts of men grow stronger
as they break before their
brothers in the faith that endures...
I see Jesus washing feet.

A man walks through the doors
to his steepled soul, lost
and found, the modern prodigal...
I see Jesus weep with joy!

Hunched over a pulpit, empty
sanctuary, he pours out his love.
Intimate avoidance of hypocrisy...
I see Jesus holding his hand.

As the coffin closes, the fingers
of God clasp his spirit and
the mourners feel his presence...
I see Jesus carrying him home!

Resounding

Eyes closed in a sanctuary
resounding in worship,
resounding from him despite
the stillness of his lips,
as his heart pours out
love he has never known before!

Praise God for breaking through
the tangled strands of
weakened cords that hid
the man he wanted me
to grow into, to mature
in His simple truths!

I no longer want to seek first
the praise of men, of her
who occupies my heart of
romance, Let it all build
on humble foundations...
the love of Him who created me!

For my pride was left on
the street corner where I prayed
to myself for all to see, yet
now know the depth of the chasm
of my sinfulness. My wall
torn down, the kingdom is here!

"Blessed are the pure in heart,
for they will see God."
(Matt. 5:8)

Facing It

Exit doors always closed.
        Ironic?...No
Focused on the challenges
        ahead of me in
        a life to be sacrificed
...for my Savior!

Lineage of Man

His first breath in garden green,
within the pure creation scene,
soon his heart stained black, unclean.
Adam's separation!

Humbled, faithful, on his knees,
"Build an ark" came on the breeze,
work began. He aimed to please.
Noah's diligence!

Sacrifice your chosen son,
thought to be the chosen one,
saved by God, a new nation.
Abraham's faithfulness!

Years of labor for her hand
in the dirt of a foreign land,
tastes of love instead of sand.
Jacob's passion!

Beaten and into slavery sold,
faith, power, dominion, gold,
faces them, strong and bold.
Joseph's forgiveness!

Humbled leader of the race,
challenged power to its face,
and led them to a freedom place.
Moses' leadership!

In youthful hand he held a rock,
and warrior Giant still did mock,
until his head had been cut off.
David's power!

Words of knowledge, temple made,
valued peace more than the blade,
thanked the God to whom he prayed.
Solomon's wisdom!

In a pit, his death to come,
lions sat and the angels sung,
a miracle, it was to some.
Daniel's survival!

Faithful husband, wife's disgrace,
heard the truth in the angel's case,
a choice that changed the human race.
Joseph's obedience!

On a cross he chose to die,
someday we will know the reason why
He so loves both you and I.
Jesus' sacrifice!

Faithful followers he did kill,
until he stepped into God's will,
evangelizing, even still.
Paul's salvation!

Men of God can do as much,
fight, love, have faith as such,
while leaning on a savior crutch.
Man's opportunity!

Psalms 139: 13-16 - A lyric

Lord, sweet hosanna, from the dusts of heaven You
formed my soul, from your image glorious.
Perfect beauty, inside human fragility, weakness, humility,
perfect love in an innocent heart.

Complexities beyond my simple mind, molded, formed,
sewn together with inspired intensity, ferocious love.
Yet in the unbeknownst serenity of the womb,
perfect love in a growing heart.

Hallelujah, Hallelujah, the gift of every breath,
fueling a fire, passion, and understanding. Deep respect, Deep awe.
For my God is truly an awesome God and
I am engulfed in the raging flood, oh the power of Him!

My spirit sits quietly, anxiously, waiting for the call.
A soulful instinct to wait. God knows...God knows...
where I wait, where I am destined to,
when the time will come, how long that time will be.

Oh God knows...God knows, it is written,
and I dare not attempt to understand, to comprehend
His wishes, His purposes, His love...the potential of me,
perfect love in an ordained heart.

"For you created my inmost being;
you knit me together in my mother's womb.
I praise you because I am fearfully and wonderfully made;
your works are wonderful,
I know that full well.

My frame was not hidden from you
when I was made in the secret place.
When I was woven together in the depths of the earth,
your eyes saw my unformed body.
All the days ordained for me
were written in your book
before one of them came to be."
(Psalms 139:13-16)

Pastor Man

A thought today occurred to me
of my faithful pastor and that he
cannot make the same mistakes as me
and how heavy that pressure must be
to be a shepherd for God!

The Wind

Today the wind ran its
fingers through my hair
and it felt like God
holding me to his chest.

The grass waved as
His holy robe brushed
the surface of the field
as Jesus walked with me.

And when I turned my back
on the breeze, to go my own
way...it kept blowing, whispering
always there, He is always there.

God draws near and I pull away.
Pride, ego, masculinity?
It seems maybe that man's intimacy fears
are not limited to women.

I try to love the wind!

Quiet Time

In the word a verse speaks out...
text emblazoned in my eyes
filled with tears flowing down
upon God-breathed words formed and sewn
with guidance firm, guidance wise.

A bluebird sings from my windowsill.
Gideon here with blue feathered wings.
upon outside breezes into my room...
confirming words from God do loom...
over my spirit which begins to sing...

Seek ye first His kingdom come.
Press on towards the goal, the prize.
Do not worry over the hairs of your head,
I am the Way, the Truth, Jesus said...
so I may finally see with my eyes.

...the resonance of quiet time...

Luke 11:33 - A Lyric

Where I am today is bright
with sun reflecting off the page,
the snow, the trees, and ice...
and possibly from me as well.
For the Son he did ignite
my soul when to Him I
ran, to Him I prayed
to radiate like Moses
with the glory of Him
who made man...and
made him *a man*
who honors the Father above
and exposes darkened worlds
to pure light and truth.

"No one lights a lamp and puts it in a place
where it will be hidden, or under a bowl.
Instead he puts it on its stand, so that those
who come in may see the light."
(Luke 11:33)

Part 5 - Eve and Love Revisited

The time has come to face
the lessons learned and see her
in colors from heaven's palette
and rejoice in the image and
companionship of Eve.

The Puzzle Piece

All of creation is a jigsaw puzzle
set before God.
I am but a small piece on the edge
of this grander scheme.
As youthful puzzle pieces tend to do
I tried in vain...
To fit into the most attractive spot
which I thought...
Was in the center of it all, next to
another young piece...
Whose pronounced, strengthened edges and
retracted, weakened areas
simply did not quite fit despite
all my efforts.
God removed me and set me off
to the side...
Where I realized my identity in His
picture of life.
I allowed myself to be picked up by
His loving hand.
I watched and looked in amazement and joy
as He placed...
me where all my rough edges fit and
my colors blended...
Where my strengths filled weakened gaps
in surrounding pieces...
and my weaknesses too were met with
strength and love.
Surrounding me now were pieces of beauty,
blessings and promise.
Images of faith, future, camaraderie all
bridged with me.
So too did an image of her with
beauty and grace.

Her weakest points matched brilliantly
with my strengths.
My weakest points overcome by
her perfect strengths.
Thank you God for my place of
humility in life...
And the indescribable blessings of your
renewal and guidance.
Truly you are a God of love,
mercy and grace!

She Exists

She exists, the woman of dreams
her eyes, shining with hope,
her smile, spreading, inspiring joy
in those who cross her path.
Her mind, emitting thoughts intriguing and deep.
Her laughter lights up the world.

She exists, the woman, oh the woman,
her hair, a velvet curtain,
her skin, satin to the touch,
soft, so soft and gentle.
Her hands, always speaking, telling,
sharing what she is feeling, thinking, and needing.

She exists, the woman who inspires me,
beautiful, intelligent, mysterious,
she exists in all women
yet all women are unique.
None worthy of pain and sadness,
all worthy of joy and love.

Her Morning, Her Awakening

Morning, dawn, awakening, early,
arising, dressing, quiet, exhausted,
debating, deeply, reminded, convinced,
leaving, cold, walking, jogging,

thinking, worrying, anxious, sigh,
challenges, obstacles, flooding, overwhelming,
breathing, deeply, reminded, convinced,
arriving, warming, choosing, beginning,

energy, bursting, heart, pumping,
fears, forgotten, worries, dropped,
freeing, deeply, reminded, convinced,
arriving, joy, spirit, smile,

driven, pushing, going, going,
pain, invigorating, developing, strengthening,
growing, deeply, reminded, convinced,
focusing, burning, lungs, soul,

slowing, wincing, soon, soon,
threshold, close, passed, joy,
ready, deeply, reminded, convinced,
stopping, fulfilled, strong, beautiful!

Pressing Glass

Pressing glass, her breath a misty cloud
escaping the warmth that she is,
escaping into the cold mountain morning.
The dawn brightens over the eastern peaks.

Snow fell overnight, deep, soft powder.
She may have slept, but her heart never rested,
excited, anxious, yearning for the mountain.
The gondola begins to move.

She is carried up the mountain, her soul rising,
racing the sun towards the summit.
A blank canvas of white between her feet below.
The summit comes into view...heart pounding.

At the top of the run she pauses,
held by something unseen, yet powerful,
demanding her to let go of her worries.
They are blown away by the mountain breeze.

She pushes off, begins her journey
blazing her own trail through the purity,
the snow, the life laid before her by God.
The sun, risen, ignites the snow.

The slope is illuminated in gleaming white,
she weaves through trees, open spaces, past obstacles ominous.
Driven to make the run clean, perfect, adventurous.
The mountain cheers her on.

Steepness subsides, she reaches the base.
Turning, she looks up at the single track winding
through perils and joy to where she now stands.
A tear and a smile, her spirit is free!

Prodigal's Sister

She is overjoyed at the sight
      of him in the driveway...home again!
        Sister of the Prodigal Son!

Rhetoric of Her

The persuasion began in her youth.
Fighting, debating the masses for truth, for
respect, each day an appeal, a battle
against the fallacy of her stereotype. Invention.

Logos takes hold of her spirit.
Ignorance drowns in a deep sea of revelation.
Molding, building, forming, sculpting,
proud, beautiful, woman, young woman. Arrangement.

Exposure of her mind, expansion of her soul.
Challenging the expectations, the insinuations,
man's world pressure, feminine heart, feminine power.
Ethos, Pathos, ever-present Logos! Style.

Wisdom gained through triumphs and trials,
support to persuade, support for her truth,
the truth in a world of fallacious discourse.
A smile, a serenity, passion prepared. Memory.

At last she speaks, her life rhetoric
commanding, demanding, penetrating steel hearts.
A woman, beautiful and strong. A mind
brilliant. The world takes notice, persuaded. Delivery.
The rhetoric of her!

Dream Girl

Nighttime clouds float past the moon
on winds that whisper lullabies
and pick her up where she will soon
appear before my dream-filled eyes.

A journey made each sleepy night
across the miles between
into my mind in sleep's twilight
where nightly she is seen.

Her Song

Echoes deep within her mind, heart pounding,
nerves firing, igniting the ancient instinct to run, to hide.
She stands.
The stage, overlooking the masses...her audience.

A debut of her spirit, her soul, her voice,
ready, aching, demanding to be shared.
She stands poised.
Her family watches from the balcony.

The music starts, reality sets in,
her cue fast approaching, a smile, a peace.
She stands poised, tall.
Her friends, hushed in unbearable excitement, listening.

She begins to sing.

Passion, pain, love burst from deep within,
in tones pure, so pure.
She stands poised, tall, proud.
A man looks on in silent awe and admiration.

Her concert, her life, her aria
exploding in powerful rhythms, shared in harmonic duets.
She stands poised, tall, proud, a tear on her cheek.
The world entranced in her song, healed by it.

The music, always playing, bridging the gap between
our lives and her song, her heart, her joy.
She stands.
Her song goes on.

The Roses

Roses are red, warm, passionate,
A beauty crisp and vibrant, on fire.
Etching her image on my heart,
Igniting me within, the rose is love.

Violets are blue, cool, distant,
A gap, widening, deepening, saddening,
Her image, all that remains, still vivid,
Lonely for her, the violet is silence.

Speak, cry out, search for the rose!
Never let it wilt, never let it fade.
Cherish the rose for it is simple,
Admire the rose for it is joy!

The Lake

A cool, crisp summer morning, misty, foggy,
a haze obscuring the opposite shore...the lake.
Glassy, smooth, expectant, the water waits
for life to stir in it, on it, and through it.

As she looks over the lake she feels serene,
the peaceful rustle of leaves in the morning breeze.
the dock on which she stands rocks gently, imperceptibly,
she steps off.

The water envelopes her, invigorates her, welcomes her.
She swims, gently, effortlessly, quietly moving,
cutting a line between the world in which she lives
and the world that she calls home.

With each passing moment she drops her worries and fears
and they drown in the depths of the lake.
Her heart swells, she reaches shore, she breaks.
Tears pour from her soul, the joy of the lake.

The fog lifts, the sun comes out,
the lake comes to life, almost as if it knew...
knew that she needed her time, knew she needed peace,
knew that her soul longed to swim.

She and He

Innocent, young, searching for direction, she
grows, matures, feels stronger, yet still weak, she
sees, feels, a hole, a void, a deep longing, a need, she
searches while not searching, looks while not looking, she

meets someone, tall, strong, searching for direction, he
opens up, shares his soul, makes her smile, he
is nervous, his void also deep, needing to be filled, he
hopes, dreams, for her, to be with her, he

develops courage, asks her, anxiously waits, she
is speechless, excited, nervous, overjoyed, she
knows he fills her void, not perfectly but, she
knows he's perfect enough, strong enough, she

says yes, to the journey, the adventure, he
smiles, she smiles, they cry, they embrace, they
feel full, complete, ready for life abundant, they
are in deep, true, passionate love.

Ephesians 5:22-24 - A Lyric

Oh wives, glorious women strong and kind,
patient are you, devoted, sweet love
for your Creator in heaven who delights
in the purity, in the excitement of your praise!

So be it that your men were designed, created
with the need for your praise, your respect. Fighting
always for your love, your faithful belief in them.
Your happiness and satisfaction, a deep instinct of man.

Formed with the strength of God they
pursue battles, in life, to defend you and to advance you,
with Christ-like aggression and Christ-like service,
washing, admiring the feet of you, the beauty!

For you, oh wives, oh church, your praise and submission to God,
ignites His heart, drives Him to give more, be more.
So it is with your husbands, by God's perfect design.
Let them lead, let them love, truly. Let them be men...

Your hearts and your lives will be blessed!

*"Wives, submit to your husbands as to the Lord.
For the husband is the head of the wife as Christ
is the head of the church, his body, of which
he is the Savior.
Now as the church submits to Christ, so also wives
should submit to their husbands in everything."*
(Eph. 5:22-24)

Late Autumn

It is cold, bitter cold, the sun obscured by clouds.
What was green, now faded and speckled with snow,
the leaves blowing here and there,
flashes of brown, orange, and gold.
The world is quiet, winter is a solemn time approaching.

We prepare for patience, shorter days, colder days.
Dreams of fires crackling and the gentle warmth...
Lovers grow close, an ancient instinct, survive.
Hold each other, gaze, warm the body, ignite two hearts.

The coldest of seasons, the warmest of loves.
Love formed truly by nature, by God.
The sun not visible in the sky, but shining in two souls,
how sweet the winter will be!

Modern Prodigal

Upon that day within my youth
I pondered there awhile
between myself and imparted truth
from father soon beguiled.

A claim I made for my due heirs
my independence sought
not knowing of the whens or wheres
I asked him for my lot.

Disappointed, though with tearful nod
he sent me on my way
distance gained with each step I trod
pursuing my glory day.

My back toward home and cognizance
a trail of muddied brick
filled with self-omnipotence
without a walking stick.

I found myself within the woods
with deep undergrowth about
but never did I think I should
return to father's house.

Through the woods my blade did slice
as I neared the foreign edge
a glimpse of flowered meadows enticed
me to an unknown ledge

A pause to think of how to cross
a canyon deep and wide
where echoes start and then are lost
before reaching the other side

Flowered meadows still were seen
across the gaping void
and there she sat and called to me
with whom she flirted...toyed.

So taken was I that I made the leap
of which success had no hope
I landed hard and in a heap
as she lowered down a rope.

A rope I climbed so willingly
upon her given terms
my heart I gave unwittingly
with yet a lesson learned.

I followed her in the foreign land
ignoring my homesick woes
and all my dreams fell from my hand
and shattered 'neath her toes.

To heal my hurts I sought the gold
and ate of meals grand
Yet found I did not fit the mold
and scarcely could I stand.

Joyful moments mixed with pain
and longing for embrace
despite her love she felt not the same
and tears rolled down my face.

As years passed by I returned to the ledge
and thought of father's home
and through my thoughts I did dredge
so sad to feel alone.

It was then my wounded heart withdrew
and deemed I'd gone to far
with boldness I had hardly knew
I told her of my scars.

Of my need to feel my father's grace
I spoke to her no lie
Her anger it did fill that place
Where now her eyes do cry.

Slowly I made plans to go
back to my father's home
three times I sought for her to go
yet she made me go alone.

As I left in faith a prayer I said
to drink of forgiving milk
I approached the canyon and the ledge
to find a bridge was built.

Made from logs within the woods
a trail now was cleared
undergrowth that be present should
rather had been sheared.

I sat and rested there in shade
and picked a fruit to eat
there I wept in wooded glade
for mercy, it is sweet.

Shortly I began again
as home drew ever near
prepared to tell him of my sin
should my father lend an ear

My healing heart prepared to serve
in the fields of his grace
upon my knees to till his dirt
for deserving so my place.

As I stepped out from the woods
a familiar path I found
running now I knew I could
for this was solid ground.

On a hill a roof I saw
and recognized it for my own
a smile grew across my jaw
at the sight of father's home.

Soon I saw a cloud of dust
swirling from the road
from it emerged my father just
as I dropped my heavy load.

From a short distance away
my speech I began to share
but there he did embrace the day
and me, his long lost heir.

The words I had prepared were tossed
for I could not make a sound
as he cried, "My son was lost,
but now my son is found!"

About the Author

Richard "Rick" Rapp was born on October 5th, 1979 in Denver, Colorado. A lifelong native of the, "Mile High" state, he grew up in the suburbs of Denver involving himself primarily in school and athletics. He accepted Jesus Christ as his personal Savior at the age of nine, but did not truly understand this commitment until a high school youth group mission trip to Juarez, Mexico. On that trip he was exposed to the true faith of believers who did not live in the abundance of the United States, and it led Rick to recommit his life to Jesus Christ.

In high school Rick first discovered his love for both writing and music, with several of his short stories being published in online literary journals. A series of events led Rick to decline his collegiate acceptances after high school, which in turn led him to Fort Collins, Colorado where he met the woman he would marry less than two years later at the age of nineteen. During the marriage he distanced himself from his writing, music, and unfortunately his faith as well...to, "focus on family life."

In 2004, after five years, the marriage relationship dissolved and Rick was faced with divorce while working towards a degree in Nursing at the University of Northern Colorado. At this time he felt God leading him back to a committed faith, writing, music, and a love for the outdoors. At the same time he also felt led to pursue his passion for teaching, and changed majors to Biology / Pre-Medicine to allow the opportunity to become a biology & anatomy professor. Today Rick is pursuing his faith, writing, and college degree with refreshed perspective and a desire to share his experiences with other men and women of the faith.

Printed in the United States
31920LVS00006B/474